W9-AWF-052

VALLEY PARK
ELEMENTARY LIBRARY DISCARD

Scholastic's The Magic School Bus®

TAKING FLIGHT
A Book About Flight

SCHOLASTIC INC.
New York   Toronto   London   Auckland   Sydney

From an episode of the animated TV series
produced by Scholastic Productions, Inc.
Based on *The Magic School Bus* books
written by Joanna Cole and illustrated by Bruce Degen

TV tie-in adaptation by Gail Herman and illustrated by Carolyn Bracken.
TV script written by Kermit Frazier, George Bloom, and Jocelyn Stevenson.

No part of this publication may be reproduced in whole or in part, or stored in a retrieval system,
or transmitted in any form or by any means, electronic, mechanical, photocopying, recording,
or otherwise, without written permission of the publisher. For information regarding permission,
write to Scholastic Inc., 555 Broadway, New York, NY 10012.

ISBN 0-590-73871-2

Copyright © 1997 by Joanna Cole and Bruce Degen.
Published by Scholastic Inc.
SCHOLASTIC, THE MAGIC SCHOOL BUS, and logos are trademarks
and/or registered trademarks of Scholastic Inc. All rights reserved.

12   1 2/0

Printed in the U.S.A.   24

First Scholastic printing, June 1997

Our teacher, Ms. Frizzle, always takes us on the wildest field trips. So we knew something amazing would happen when we went to the model airplane show. We just didn't know what!

Early that morning, we all met in the schoolyard. Tim and Wanda were so excited! They had built their very own model airplane for the show. They felt sure they could win a prize for their design.

"Wow! Look at those wings!" said Arnold.

"You can't try flying a plane without them," Tim said proudly.

I think we need binoculars for this!

Try flying? Arnold hoped Ms. Frizzle hadn't heard that! But the Friz had that funny look on her face, and she was staring at the model airplane in a very interested way.

"Oh, no!" Arnold cried. "You're not thinking about a field trip in that little plane, are you, Ms. Frizzle?"

"Of course not, Arnold," Ms. Frizzle said. "I'm through thinking about it."

"Liz!" she called. "The portashrinker, please!"

Ms. Frizzle assigned Tim, Phoebe, and Liz to be the ground crew—even though Arnold really wanted to stay behind. Then she set the dial on the portashrinker and handed it to Phoebe.

The next thing we knew, we were each as small as a thumb—the perfect size for a model airplane ride.

So we climbed right on board, and buckled up our seat belts.

"The wild blue yonder is yours, Wildcat," Ms. Frizzle said. "Go for it!"

"All systems go!" Wanda called from the pilot's seat.

"Come on, Wanda," Ralphie said, "those controls aren't real."

"That's *Wildcat* Wanda to you," Wanda said.

Then Phoebe picked up the plane and flipped the propeller. *Zzzz!* The motor buzzed to life.

Tim started to work the controls. Phoebe put the plane back on the ground, and we taxied across the schoolyard. Faster . . . faster. . . . We took off from the ground.

Wheee! We were flying!

Everything was going great. "Feel that air move past us!" shouted Keesha. Ms. Frizzle smiled. "They don't call it an airplane for nothing!" she said.

Then, down on the ground, Phoebe took the controls from Tim. She pulled on the stick and lifted our nose straight up to the sky.

"I wonder how high it will go," said Phoebe.

"Uh-oh," said Keesha. "The air's not moving so fast anymore."

"We're slowing down," warned Wanda.

Dorothy Ann checked her book. "According to my research, when a plane's nose tips up and slows down like this, it's called a stall."

"Stall?" Ralphie asked nervously. "As in stop flying?!"

We hung onto our seats as the plane sank toward the ground. Quickly, Phoebe slammed the stick the other way.

Whew! The nose dipped down. We straightened out just in time!

It was almost time for the Air Show. So Tim took the controls to look for a place we could land. Tim *didn't* look where he was going, though.

"Oops!" he cried. The remote flew from his hand and smashed into little bits.

Ralphie looked down and saw the broken control. "Oh, no!" he shouted. "We're flying without Tim!"

We all yelled and screamed and cried for help. But it didn't do one bit of good. We kept flying.

Over the school . . . past our houses . . . out of town!

Good old Ralphie tried to steer us back. "Maybe this has something to do with the steering," he said, pushing down on a lever on the side of the plane.

The wings folded up flat.

"Then again, maybe not," Ralphie shouted as — *zzzzzz!* — we went sinking down!

"Get those wings back down!" ordered Wanda.

We leaned out of the plane as far as we could. Then we pushed the wings with all our might.

Click! They snapped back down. The wind whooshed over them, and we leveled out, one, two, three.

But Carlos and Dorothy Ann pushed so hard . . .

. . . they tumbled right out! They clung to the wings, waving like flags in the wind.

Arnold was confused. "If the wings are holding up the plane, what's holding up the wings?" he asked.

"Moving air!" Wanda told him. "When the air moves across the wings, it pushes us up!"

Back on the ground, Tim and Phoebe were frantic. "Hurry, Liz!" said Tim. "We have to find them! You have to turn the bus into a search-and-rescue plane!"

Liz closed her eyes and jabbed a button. *Bang! Boom! Bing!* The bus transformed into the strangest flying machine Tim had ever seen.

The wings flapped. The copter bounced up and down. *Thud!* It crumpled in a heap.

Liz tried again. This time the bus wheezed and sputtered. Then it popped into a flying machine with several long wings.

Slowly, it rose a few feet off the ground.

"All right, Liz!" cried Phoebe. "You did it!"

Again it dropped, collapsing with a hiss of steam.

This heap is way too heavy. We didn't have enough lift.

Meanwhile, Dorothy Ann and Carlos had crawled back inside the plane. But that didn't cheer up Arnold.

"Look," he said. "Our propeller just stopped turning."

The propeller kept us moving forward. If we weren't being pulled forward by the propeller, we would slow down and there would be less air moving across our wings. And when less and less air moves across our wings . . .

"What happens, class?" Ms. Frizzle asked brightly.

It was a good thing a tree was there to break our fall. We peeked out of the leaves, feeling discouraged.

"Wildcat Wanda never gives up!" Wanda said. "Think! We need to get air moving across our wings again."

Carlos frowned. "But there is no moving air, if we're not moving."

The Friz pointed out the eagle circling overhead.

"That's it!" said Wanda excitedly. "The bird can tow us!"

But once we were in the air, how would we stay up?

"A bird stays up by flapping its wings," said Arnold. "Right?"

Ms. Frizzle beamed. "Exactly. To move forward, a bird flaps its wings and a plane spins its propeller. It's the same idea."

"So how do we get the propeller to turn?" asked Carlos. Ms. Frizzle had the answer right in her bag.

We hooked up the propeller to Ms. Frizzle's unicycles, and the bird to the plane. When the bird took off, so did we!

"Start your cycles!" shouted Wanda. We all pedaled wildly.

"I've got that air-moving-over-wings feeling!" Wanda reported. "We're climbing with our own power now!"

Then Arnold crawled out to untie the bird. But once the bird was untied, he forgot to let go of the rope!

Excuse me, please.

Arnold pulled himself hand over hand onto the bird's tail.
He gripped the feathers tightly.

"Arnold!" Ms. Frizzle called. "Is the bird doing anything
with its tail?"

"It's moving back and forth in the wind. Sort of like he's
steering," Arnold said. "Maybe I can steer back to you!"

"Sounds like the proper course to me!" the Friz said.

So Arnold twisted and turned the tail as gently as he could.

The bird swooped closer to the plane. Wanda grabbed the rope—and Arnold slid back into his seat. But before poor Arnold even took a breath, we flew right into a clothesline.

The plane looped and spun and flew upside down.

We were out of control!

Meanwhile, Tim and Phoebe were still in the bus. Suddenly, the bus jerked and jolted and turned into a real flyer! It bobbed up and down, then lifted high off the ground.

"Watch out for that building!" Tim shouted.

Just in time, Liz pressed another button. The bus spun once in the air, then s-t-r-e-t-c-h-e-d into a stronger, faster plane. *Whizz!* They zoomed over the building, no problem!

We were the ones with a problem! "Too bad this plane isn't a bird, so we could steer," Arnold muttered.

"Arnold, you're a genius!" Wanda cried. "Planes have tails just like birds. They have flaps called elevators and a rudder, too. Now go out there and steer!"

Before Arnold could protest, the Friz bundled him into a windbreaker, tied him to a safety rope, and he was out on the tail! That's when we noticed all these planes buzzing around.

"Watch out!" shouted Wanda. "We're dropping fast. We need to climb. Elevators up, Arnold!"

But Arnold was so nervous he pushed down on the left elevator and up on the right one.

Oh, no! We did a triple roll with a double outside loop!

Just then, Tim and Phoebe flew near the show. "Look!" shouted Tim. "It's them. And boy, are they in trouble! Nobody's ever done a triple roll with a double outside loop!"

Liz dived into the cockpit to press another button. The bus twirled and grew and when it stopped, it was a giant plane with a landing strip on top!

I hope they see us!

Tremendous!

Amazing!

Stupendous!

We spotted Liz right away, waving us in for a landing. "Turn left," Wanda shouted to Arnold. "Remember the bird!"

Twist and turn, Arnold thought. So he moved the rudder—the piece at the very end of the plane that helps steer, too. At the same time, he raised the left elevator up, and pushed the right one down.

Yes! The wing dipped down and we banked—tilted—left.

Wanda directed Arnold left, then right, then left again. Each time, he turned the rudder or the elevator to steer the plane lower and lower.

But we all felt so tired. We'd been cycling for so long, our legs slowed down. The plane dropped faster.

Would we make it?

"Ease off the elevators!" ordered Wanda. We leveled out just in time and skidded down the runway with a screech.

After that, landing on the ground was a snap. Phoebe quickly zapped us back to normal size. But we were in for one more surprise. Tim and Wanda won the grand prize!

"Thank you," said Tim. "But this trophy belongs to everyone in our class. Right, Wanda?"

"Right," Wanda told him. "But that's Wildcat Wanda to you!"

Reporter: Congratulations on winning the grand prize. Do you mind answering some questions?

Tim: Not at all.

Reporter: Is steering a bird or plane really that easy?

Tim: Nope. Airplanes have movable flaps on the wings that help steer, too. Birds use wings for lift and a push forward. They flap so quickly — in all different directions — we can't even see the whole motion!

Reporter: Those certainly were strange-looking planes you flew earlier. Do they really exist?

Tim: Yup. The first two didn't get off the ground. But the next one, called the Wright Flyer, was the first airplane to actually stay in the air for some time, while at the same time being able to steer where it flew.

Reporter: Still, everyone knows there's no such thing as a portashrinker or a flying bus!

Tim: Maybe not. But we still won the grand prize!

- Steering a plane—or bird—is very complicated.

- Airplanes have movable flaps on the wings—as well as the tail. Pilots raise one flap up and lower the other one down. If the right flap goes up, the wing goes down—and the plane makes a banking turn to the right.

- As for birds, they use wings for lift and a push forward. They flap so quickly—in all different directions—we can't even see the whole motion!

Ms. Frizzle